The information in this book experience of Samantha Kell Twitter documentation.

First Edition

First published 2014

Copyright © 2014 Kissed Off Creations Ltd and Samantha Kelly

Written by Samantha Kelly
Edited by Natalie Ballard

Book and cover design by Natalie Ballard
for Kissed Off Publications
Tweety Bird made by Danielle Mansell
https://twitter.com/ColourMeFun
Published by Kissed Off Publications

The moral right of the Author has been asserted.

All rights reserved. No part of this publication may be reproduced or transmitted in any for or by any means, electronic or mechanical, including photocopy, recording, or any information storage and retrieval system, without permission in writing from the Publisher. Trademarks, brand names and company names mentioned belong to their respective owners.

A catalogue record for this book is available from the British Library

ISBN: 978-0-9928601-1-0

Copies for bookstores, libraries and public bodies available directly from the Publisher.

Kissed Off Publications

www.kissedoff.co.uk

Acknowledgements

Gosh where do I start? Well first of all of course I want to thank my two beautiful daughters for their patience and understanding when I am working. I am so proud of you both. Thank you for believing in me and for the love and hugs. Also a huge thank you to my partner Andy - Thank you for making me so happy and showing me the meaning of love. You are my rock and soulmate. Also by the way, without whom I wouldn't be able to go to all those meetings and the house would be a mess! lol Also, my daughters Leah and Abi.

I'd like to thank my sister Roz who set me up on Twitter in the first place and has always been my best friend even through tough times before Twitter changed my life.

My sister Rachel and her partner Audrey for putting me up when I had to go to Dublin for workshops and meetings!

My brother David and my Mum for helping me out financially when I started my first business Funky Goddess. None of this would've been possible without their support. My Dad for teaching me to work hard but be kind to others and help out when I can. Miss you so much.

My sister Linda and brother Vinnie for their support.

Leonie for helping me out by minding my children and the dogs.

The fellowship. My wonderful friends who are also in recovery, thank you.

Irishbizparty - This community is a wonderful positive community. The fact that everyone takes part every week is the reason it is so successful. Thank you all for your support

Locally here in Wexford, Thanks to Julie O Neill, George Lawlor, Brendan Ennis, Tony Ennis and Fred Karlsson, Pat Mc Cormack, Damian Donlon, who listened and supported me when I couldn't get any support starting off. Thank you for believing in me.

Bill Liao for being very patient and for having faith in me and telling me 'You ARE good enough'

My wonderful Twitter followers… there are so many it's impossible to include you all, so please don't be offended if you're not mentioned… I love you all!! Special thanks to Barbara Scully, Maria Duffy, Norah Bohan, Miriam Donohoe, Marissa Carter, Gareth O Connor, Paul Dunphy, Noel Cuddy, Joe Lawlor, Lilliwhiterose, Sharon Lawless, Michelle Duffy. Susan Hayes, Aidan O Carroll, Chris Mc Gillycuddy, Linda Flynn, Jagdeep Sahans, Helena Tubridy, Linda Shackleford, Anita Whyte, Joanne Sweeney Burke, Fionnuala Mc Auley, Mark from Radio Active and Lyndon Wood who gave me a chance. To all of my followers: some of your Tweets and messages have made all the difference to my life on Twitter especially during 'Troll' times.

Thank you Dragons Den and RTE especially Alan Robinson who filmed 'She's the business' and thanks to Independent.ie and Ailish O Hora for your support. Also thank you Colm Hayes of 2fm who helped me by taking my call that day I launched Funky Goddess. Getting on air can make such a difference to a start up. Thank you also TV3 for having me on Boost my business.

Thank you to Natalie Ballard and Carol Faughnan who helped me put this book together. Carol, I would be lost without you sometimes!!

How important is Social Media for business?

Essential I would say! Twitter especially is my forte. I didn't even know how to turn on a computer when I started Funky Goddess two years ago. I discovered that I had a knack with Twitter and have built up a great following on *@Tweetinggoddess* just from targeting the right people and interacting with them daily. I'm not mad about Facebook especially with all the new rules but depending on your market and your business it is great for getting attention also. LinkedIn and Google+ I am still getting the hang of to be honest! I advocate the use of all social systems but make sure they fit your overriding social strategy to leverage them properly.

How did you become an Entrepreneur?

It was both necessity and a desire to go for it. I saw a gap in the market for girls who were approaching the awkward milestone of their first period and I thought that this was a great way to help girls my daughter's age and Mums and Dads too. I thought 'why isn't there something to help with this awkward phase...' and then thought, 'OK I will do something about it!' So I created Funky Goddess. (I have since sold the business and it is still going strong under new owners).

Can you tell us about your Dragon Den experience?

It was amazing, I got so much exposure from it and met all the Dragons who were just human beings after all! Everyone was lovely on the set and it gave me a real insight into how to do a pitch too. If you can pitch to a panel of Dragons you can pitch anywhere! It was an exciting experience but also an emotional one as my Dad and I used to watch it all the time. He passed away a few months before - he would have been so proud.

Advice for anyone thinking of setting up a business

Go for it! Get yourself out there, tell anyone who will listen to you about what you do. Surround yourself with positive people and don't' be afraid to ASK for assistance from more experienced business mentors. I give talks to Women's groups on how to get noticed and top tips for using Twitter also. So this goes down very well. Don't be afraid to let your personality shine through either it worked for me!.

This book also contains the stories of other Twitter users.

This photo is of Fionnuala from Scarecrow Flowers who I met on Twitter, she made this dress out of flowers, came to the conference in Dublin and made the front page of national newspapers as a result!! We are now great friends... and all through Twitter. Fionnuala is *https://Twitter.com/scarecrowflower*

The photo is taken by David Mc Auley photography. I met David on Twitter and he has always supported *#Irishbizparty* and often takes pictures for us. Find him at *https://Twitter.com/DMcAPhotography*.

Tweet Your Way to Success

Guide your business to success in 140 characters

Tweeting Quick Tips

- Twitter username should be similar to your Brand
- Follow those who would be interested in what you do/have to offer
- Tweet interesting tweets…it's all about content!
- Re-Tweet others
- Avoid controversy
- If you are an SME… Be yourself… bring your personality into your tweets
- Enjoy it! Through Twitter, people have assisted me to change my life, and I have in turn been able to be of greater service to them… there is a whole new world out there just waiting to hear from you!
- Interact, Interact, Engage, Engage
- Follow active Tweeters, journalists etc

Introduction

Twitter has changed my life. Through Twitter, people have assisted me to change my life and I have in turn been able to be of greater service to them.

Before I knew about Twitter my life had become unmanageable. I wasn't a happy camper… was ambling along in life. Got myself into a few dodgy relationships and was also dangerously fond of the demon drink. I had a daughter who I'd brought up by myself due to divorce from her Dad and was in my second marriage with a man who I loved but there was something missing. I had another daughter who is hearing impaired so I was her carer at the time. My world was a constant wheel of taking her to speech therapy appointments, Mammy duties of school runs and to be honest as I wasn't from the area where I was living I was very lonely. I was frustrated with the constant struggle and having no money.

I started to lean on alcohol and find solace there a bit more. I realised that perhaps there was a problem too as I noticed it was when I was feeling lonely or angry that I craved it. I drank alone too as I couldn't go out as I didn't have any friends to go out with, or the friends I did have certainly didn't drink as much as I did so I wasn't going to hang out with them and let them see how much I was drinking! So alone I drank. It was only every Friday night but that was enough to make me so hungover on the next day that I couldn't do anything really. I was sick and really tired. This went on for two days not just one the older I got.

So one day I found myself going to AA and have been sober ever since (6 years now) I go to meetings regularly and I have wonderful friends in the fellowship. So that was when my life started to turn around.

I was hitting 40, Abi was about to start in primary school. Also my marriage wasn't happy and we were both just trundling along. My Dad has just passed away and I was devastated. I loved my Dad so much. He was so kind and in his own little way a bit of a Del Boy and Entrepreneur. He always taught us to work hard and save money and never to take things on credit too. He always said to me 'Sam, if we could just think of one simple thing to invent we could be millionaires'. He was our 'Homer', he didn't always get it right but he was our guide and our softie but wouldn't like to be in trouble with him as he was scary when he was angry with you! I knew if he called me Samantha instead of Sam I was in BIG trouble! This didn't happen often though especially as he got older and the grandchildren came along. He mellowed a bit and just wanted peace and quiet. His pipe, cup of tea and to sit and watch the birds on his bird table.

So I was wondering what was life all about... life was too short... what had I done exactly? I know I had two amazing girls who I adored this was my best achievement. But what if they wanted to go to college? We had never been on a sun holiday or been able to get things that most kids had and I didn't want them going without. I wanted the best for them especially as in the meantime Leah was diagnosed with diabetes type 1 and now both of them had stuff to contend with in their own lives.

So one day I was in the supermarket. My eldest who was 11 at the time had just got her first period. Now this subject is a bit of a taboo at the best of times but I felt so sorry for her that I thought 'I know, I will go down and get her a starter set with everything she needs in it and some nice girly stuff too'... but I was amazed to discover that there were none! I said to myself 'now hang on a sec... why not?' So that was the moment that Funky Goddess was born.

I did a bit of research on the internet and decided that I was going to go for it. By this stage my marriage had broke down and we were separated. So I only had the carers allowance of €230 per week. I had no money but needed money to start my business. So I asked my Mum and anyone I knew who might have a bit of a loan to help me get started. I sourced the stock on the internet and my sister and I came up with the name 'Funky Goddess' so she helped me trade mark it and register the domain name and all that stuff that I really hadn't a clue about!

My sister Roz also made me a website as that is what she does. So I was all set! Next I needed to tell people about it.

So I started to use Facebook and then Roz set me up on Twitter. I hadn't a clue what I was supposed to do but just tweeted my first tweet:

'Excited about the new website'. That was it. And the rest they say… is history… join me on my journey and I will tell you **how I went from 0 to 13k in 140 characters**.

Hope you enjoy it!

Part 1
Starting Your Biz!

I started my first business in 2011. It was a first period gift box for girls who came to that awkward milestone in their lives. I saw there was a gap in the market and no 'beginners set' for young girls who reached puberty. So it made sense to me as a Mum. But how do you decide that your business is a viable one? I've put a little guide here based on my own experience.

There is nothing more exciting than deciding to start a business. It's also scary, stressful, nerve wrecking and daunting. But once you make the decision to do it, what's the next step?

FIRST THINGS FIRST

Right, you have had enough of the boss telling you what to do and you know you do your job well. Time to move on and set up by yourself. So... where do you start?

First to register the business go to the company registrations office or a company formation company and they will do it all for you! Always a good idea to register the business before someone else does.

Useful contacts (Ireland)

- *http://www.cro.ie/*
- *http://www.enterprise-ireland.com/en/*
- *http://www.patentsoffice.ie/*

Starting Your Biz!

- Is there a market? Do your market research. Will customers move to you from your competitor if you have one? If they don't is there enough business to sustain a living from? (If not more)

- Register the business.
  (Try *www.registerabusiness.ie* they help with the company formation side of things in Ireland, or Companies House in the UK. Equivalent institutions exist for other countries)

- Think about what you will be taking on. (No paid holidays, no ringing in sick, etc..). Make a list according to your proposed business model.

- What have you got to offer that is unique or better than others? What is your **Unique Selling Point**?

- Talk to your family members and let them know what your plans are. Involve them in the process - even the kids!

- What will your brand/company name be?

- Buy the domain name. You might not need a website now, but you will later on.

- Trade mark your brand name (or patent the idea if you need to).

Useful contacts (UK)

- *http://www.companieshouse.gov.uk/*
- *http://www.hmrc.gov.uk/startingup/*
- *http://www.ipo.gov.uk*

- If the business is a taxi company for example, get a phone number that is easy to remember when a customer has had a few drinks! You can go to a mobile phone store and ask for a good number, they are usually happy to assist.

- Create a Twitter account and Facebook page... depending on your target market. Where are they hanging out? Find out. Whatever brand you use, see is that Twitter name available. **Put your brand into the Twitter name.**

- Create a LinkedIn profile also. Put in as much detail as possible. You can do this as an individual as well as a company!

- Talk to other Entrepreneurs or business owners who you **trust**. Run it by them, seek advice. Ask for assistance. You will get to feel who best understands your business and you as an individual.

- How will you survive financially at the beginning? It take s a while for the word to spread and for you to build a reputation so make sure you have funds to keep you going at the start.

- Finally...

MAKE THE DECISION.... AND THEN GO FOR IT!!

There you are waiting for people to walk through the door or waiting for the phone to ring? Why? Nothing will happen if you just sit there and wait.

First of all, you need to get out and do something. There are several ways to do this:

1. Are you meeting and telling people about your business? Are you attending events, meet ups, networking etc.. Where might you find the customers and suppliers you need to make your business successful.

2. Are you using Social Media to get your message out there? And are you communicating that message effectively for that platform?

3. Are you building relationships with others in business so that people will support you with retweets, etc.. when you need them most?

4. Is your branding right? Is your tagline attracting the attention you need?

5. Are you targeting the right market? Who **IS** your target market? You need to establish this first.

6. Are you using the right medium to promote your business? If your target market is nationwide and global, there is no point in putting an ad in the local paper. You could get social media marketing for a month for almost the same price!

7. Are your target market people who would listen to the radio? If your target market is professionals you should be listening to the right radio show. No point in listening to local radio if your target market is elsewhere. Keep an ear out - what are people talking about?

8. Is there a way that you can get on the radio without paying for an ad? Try a press release that grabs attention. E.g. if you are in the health business can you write an article about it and send it to radio or press? They are always looking for new stories especially ones with statistics in them. For example, *20% of people are at risk from…* and put why your business can help.

9. Is your image right? Do you come across as approachable and would people like to ring you or would they feel intimidated by you or your brand? Try to think of you and how YOU would feel. Would YOU ring you?

10. Get out there, shout about it, tell the world… **I AM HERE and ready to do business!**

Most of us starting out in business have taken the courageous step but are stuck on how to get their business noticed. Most start ups have a very limited budget so you have to be careful. I had no budget for marketing so I used Twitter and Facebook to market my business. So before you go spending a fortune try these top tips I have put together first!

- Find out who your target market listens to on the radio or watches on TV. What newspaper do they read? What magazines or social media platforms are they most likely to be on? Listen to the radio and target the talk show radio stations or ring them if you hear them talking about anything relevant to what you are doing.

- **Write a press release**. Send the press release to any radio/TV program, magazine or paper that you think would be interested in your product or service. This should be interesting with pics and have a hook or problem/crisis that you have the solution for. Add a bit of your personal story too. Follow the email/phone calls up.

- **Use Twitter**. It does depend on what market you are targeting, but me I started to use it straight away to tell people what I was doing. Actually, I shouted it. To fit what you do into 140 characters can be difficult but work on it, and include the link to your site! When you gain a certain amount of followers, you can let a bit more about you or other subjects go into your tweets. Follow business people and influencers. You want them to notice you and get on their radar.

- **Use #irishbizparty** every Wednesday night 9-11pm. Plenty of other entrepreneurs out there just like you who would love to help you get out there! Also Independent.ie have linked up with us and they feature the *#Starbiz* every week on their site.

- Get **photos** of you with well known people/personalities. Always put pictures up of anyone you meet, as people want to see who you are hanging out with!

- **Get involved** in something worthwhile like a **charity** that is close to your heart. Promote and shout about it as it will help raise awareness for the charity and show people that you are human and have a heart. People like to get to know who they are dealing with. Charities need help always to raise awareness and to promote them. Also, listen to other start ups and assist them with retweets or spreading the word about what they are doing. That way they are more likely to do the same.

- Carry **business cards**, everywhere!! Give them to anyone you chat to, tell the world or anyone who will listen about what you do, and who you are! Or wear a tee shirt with your name on it!! (Walking advertisement)

- **Go** to as many places where your target market hangs out. Let them know you are there!

- **Blog** about what you do, make it interesting so people will share it for their friends to see. Show yourself as the **Expert** in what you do!

- **Dress differently** or wear warm colours or colours that suit your personality! Make an effort to stand out.
- Use **consistent** pictures and branding tools across the net so people can relate all the information they come across to you, like the same headshot, tag line for instance.
- **Ask for help** from more experience business people. If you ask, business leaders are usually happy to assist you with advice or just pointing you in the right direction

Networking for Beginners

Right so you've decided that you are going to attend a networking event. Great!!

We go to networking events to create:

- Leads
- Contacts
- Opportunities
- Meetings

Ensure you have a strategy every time you go to an event. **Who** do you want to meet... and what can YOU do for them? Networking works both ways.

"The successful networkers I know, the ones receiving tons of referrals and feeling truly happy about themselves, continually put the other person's needs ahead of their own."
- Bob Burg

BENEFITS OF NETWORKING

- Networking always creates **opportunities**. You just never know who you are going to meet!!

- **Sharing knowledge:** Some people know about grants available etc. that others wouldn't be aware of for example. Something like funding entitlements can make all the difference to a business starting out.

- **Connections:** Even if I don't necessarily have a need for your product or service, I have family, friends, sisters, brothers, nieces, nephews etc. who might!

- The people in that room will help you **promote** your service, by word of mouth after meeting you, to people OUTSIDE of the room.

- **Building relationships.** Even if you meet someone once, keep in touch, by Social media or email... check in and see how they are doing. Is there an event coming up that might interest them? Tell them about it! I met three people for the first time ever at an event recently who I had regular contact with on Twitter! Nice to put faces to the names.

WHAT CAN YOU CONTRIBUTE?

Networking has many benefits, not the least of which are the great people you will come to build relationships with. It really makes for a pleasant experience.

I personally enjoy this and have developed many great friendships. It's always nice to have friends who have your back. One lady who I met for only the second time,(she is in touch with me regularly on Facebook and Twitter), told me never to be stuck if I need a bed for the night or get stranded on the road if I am in the area! Wow, now there is a kind offer. She told me not to waste money on a hotel!

A couple of points of caution:

As you build your network of contacts and friends, always think about what **YOU** can contribute and how you can make things better for others. If you are great on Social Media for example, could you help them out by setting them up on Twitter? Or offer some tips on who to follow etc.?

Although… Guard against spending TOO much time on social networking sites, find a balance and keep your most important projects in focus. (It's a bit different for me, Social Media is my work so I will be on it much more than you will)

Networking is so essential for business. But are you networking the right way? It's not all about sell, sell, sell. Networking is all about **building relationships**. Build a network of people around you who are positive and willing to assist.

But what about you? Are you assisting others or just out to get what you can?

Here are some tips I picked up on my journey from the likes of Bill Liao, (*@Liaonet*) Susan Hayes (The positive Economist) (*@Susanhayes_*) and Ted Rubin (*@TedRubin*)

Ask yourself when you meet someone new at an event:

What is it I can do for you and who can I connect you with?

Don't forget the business card you usually get into your hand is also a person... this person will be looking for leads, connections etc. So build up a relationship with them.

- ➤ What is it I can do for you?
- ➤ Who can I connect you with?
- ➤ Is there an event happening soon that I can invite this person to?
- ➤ Leverage your connections
- ➤ Who do I know that might be able to assist you?
- ➤ Push yourself out of your comfort zone.
- ➤ You just don't know how close you can be to the right connection.

Listen to what other people have to say. Are you really listening or are you dying for your chance to speak? Ted Rubin is quick to point out 'Listening' as being important.

Follow up... ensure you follow up after events, connect online, email etc.

Right, ready? Off you go now. Build those relationships and be amazing!

TIPS FOR STRESSED OUT ENTREPRENEURS

Being an entrepreneur is a roller coaster. There are wonderful ups... and then there are the downs... the supplier who lets you down, the cashflow problems, hassle from your nearest and dearest to stop talking about your business, no support from Government bodies is a big one and one I often hear about. I have actually heard a few stories now of others robbing ideas too. This can deflate an entrepreneur so much and drive them to the edge. This is why I created *#irishbizparty* - so that we could all assist one another and even if it's just a listening ear this can help so much!

Most Entrepreneurs would admit that the **stress** of owning your own business never really outweighs the advantages and excitement of it all... But if it is getting too much for you... it might be time to look at your business properly and see where the stress is coming from.

You are getting anxious, can't sleep, want to burst into tears.

- Stop. Ask yourself… Why are you feeling like this?
- Take things a day at a time - don't try to do everything at once.
- When you start to feel stressed, take time out, close the laptop. Get out of the house or office, sit in the garden, make a cup of tea, eat some chocolate!
- Learn something new to improve your mind or do something out of your comfort zone.
- Do a good deed for someone else! When we help someone else it can take our minds off ourselves. And make us feel grateful too for things we actually **DO** have in our lives.
- Save yourself from 2 pests: Hurry and indecision
- Improve your environment. You would be amazed how a bit of a makeover or tidy up can improve your mood.
- Talk to someone. Share what is bothering you with someone who is experienced or has had the same types of challenges.
- Ask… **ask for help** if it all gets too much. There are plenty of people who would be happy to sit down and have a coffee with you and lend an ear.
- Stick with **positive people**. Stay away from the negative ones.

On the other hand… ask yourself why is your business making you feel like this? Are there reasons to look at your business and what is really going on?

The first step in determining what you should do if your business is struggling is to assess whether you have a "good business" to begin with! Whether you're running a business that's been around for five years or one that's been around for a month, it's important to take an **honest** look at what you have. It's sad to say, but some businesses shouldn't have been started in the first place, and some businesses that were great at the beginning can have a short sell by date or be doomed to failure due to lack of potential for upscaling or poor management, or both.

IS IT TIME TO MAKE AN HONEST SELF ASSESSMENT OF YOUR BUSINESS?

Remember, owning a business isn't easy, if it was, everyone would be doing it!

- Has the business taken a turn in a direction that we don't have the equipment or skills to move with?

- Has your competitor got more business than you because they are better? Do you think it is time to admit defeat?

- Are you still making money or are the margins squeezed to a point that its impossible to make money on the bottom line

- Do we have the right team behind us?

- Should we be looking at a different part of the market?

OPTIONS

Some options could be:

- Close the business
- Downsize the business
- Sell the business
- Change the market focus
- Upgrade the manufacturing capabilities
- Upgrade the senior management, etc..

The *Key* here is to do **something**

Remember, if the business fails... it doesn't mean that you have failed.

"Don't worry about failure; you only have to be right once." —Drew Houston, Dropbox founder and CEO

If none of these things apply then perhaps you are just having a bad day and you need a little break!

Take action. Stop procrastinating... **do something**. Remember the reasons you set up in business in the first place. Your family need you. So make sure that stress isn't taking over... you are no use to them if you make yourself ill.

HOW YOU CAN LEARN FROM MISTAKES I'VE MADE IN BUSINESS

I started a business back in October 2011 called Funky Goddess. I had no finance or experience but even so, I managed to get my business off the ground and into over 100 retail outlets nationwide. I sold the business in May.

However, mistakes were made, so I would like to share with you some of those mistakes in order to prevent someone else making the same.

- Try to do as much as you can from home. Avoid moving into a unit for as long as possible.

- Get your price point right at the start. It is better to start at a bigger price then bring it down afterwards if you have to. See what competitors are charging.

- Be careful who you confide in. Choose a successful business mentor who you know well and can trust. Don't go asking advice from everyone!

- Be honest with your business plan and finances. Don't assume your projected figures will turn out the way you planned.

- Ask for complete prices including vat when asking for quotes.

- Delay putting your product into retail shops. Stay as a website sales based business for as long as you can. Even if everyone all over the country wants you to stock it near them. You can't please everyone. Retail takes a higher percentage of your profit.

- If you must stock in retail units ask for payment upfront. You need cashflow and the bigger the retailer the longer you will have to wait for payment. Usually they pay after a month or two months.

- Buy in bulk. I didn't have the finance to do this but if I did, I would buy in bulk first. It is cheaper.

- Get your product right before you start selling. I changed the box after a year and it was much better and cheaper to put together. Could've saved myself a lot of hassle if I'd gone for proper branding I was happy with in the first place.

- Don't go too big before you can supply the goods. Unfortunately my idea was so popular I couldn't keep up with demand!

- Patent your idea if you can. Although mine couldn't be patented, do if you can straight away. If it is a good idea, others will think so too.

- Go for it, but Think, Think, Think about every major decision you make. Get advice from a trusted source. You are on one of the biggest roller coasters of your life! Enjoy the journey!

Courage, Determination and positivity

The recession has made things tough for a lot of us. People are hanging on to what little money they have. You wonder sometimes, why am I doing this? The unpredictability of not knowing whether you will have money from one week to the next is one of the disadvantages of being your own boss.

I started *Tweeting Goddess* in July. So it's still early days for me. Word of mouth and brand awareness are how I am advertising what I do. I use Twitter and other forms of social media to promote what I do as I don't have a marketing budget. I am lucky that I have a big network I can tap into as I have built up many wonderful relationships along the way since my first start up.

Courage

But imagine if you were starting up today, in a recession from scratch. Starting a business is scary, fun, exciting, crazy and a mind blowing Roller Coaster! You need **courage** to start a business. There is nothing 'normal' about getting up, getting out there and taking a risk that you are starting something that might not take off at all.

I know the stresses that can be involved when starting up. I am well aware of how lonely a place it can be. There are many who are willing to offer assistance if you have the courage to ask. So there it is again… Courage… it takes courage to ask for help.

Determination

I have come across many obstacles on my journey. Finance being the biggest one. (or lack of it). Also, childcare, lack of connections, experience etc.. I have been put down by trolls, by others who can't stand me for some reason and been targeted by begrudgers. But I kept going, kept coming back, kept smiling, kept at it. That is **determination**... belief in what I do and my abilities to do what I love in a way that will help others to become bigger and better. By passing on my knowledge and experience to others, this has helped me and kept me even more determined!

Positivity

When anything good happens in my life or in my work, I tell everyone about it! I shout it from the rooftops, I embrace the **positive**. I surround myself with like minded people who are also positive. I stay away from anyone who makes me feel like *'I need to get away from this person, they are wrecking my head'*.

Reaching out

But what about you? Have you spotted an entrepreneur who may be struggling and need an extra helping hand? Lots of us have skills and expertise to give so why not do a good thing today and reach out to that entrepreneur and ask them for a coffee?

Starting Your Biz!

You love that you are your own boss! Whoop Whoop!

You tell anyone who will listen, how great your business idea is

You get used to driving around with the petrol gauge on 'E'

You won't take a sick day!

Your other half will be sick of hearing about your business idea!

You will have done something that many would love to do but didn't do for various reasons. Well done!

You will wonder what it is like to know when your pay day is

Most of the time a start up hasn't even got the money for a coffee! Now that you are in a better position, perhaps you could buy them a coffee or lunch, have a chat and see if there is any way you can assist?

It could be a contact that you know who might make a big difference. Or a skill that they mightn't have or be aware that they have, that they aren't using.

Every start up needs *courage, determination and positivity*. Positive traits that not everyone has. So embrace them, use them and share what you have with someone else. One day it **WILL** come back to you.

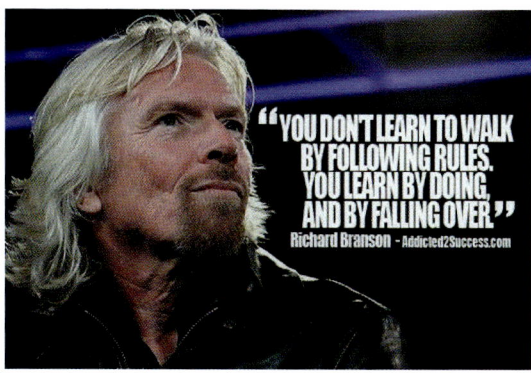

You will stop watching the Simpsons and start watching the business news

You will learn to surround yourself with supporters and ignore begrudgers

Your family will want a conversation with you someday that has nothing to do with your business!

IS KINDNESS AN ESSENTIAL TRAIT OF A LEADER?

During my journey into the Business world, I have met many Business Leaders. A lot of them had that 'je ne sais quoi' I noticed. They would walk into a room and the place stands still... or... they sit quietly in the background taking everything in and noticing everything but stayed quiet. There is a magnetic attraction (no, not that type of attraction)!!

The ones that stood out for me definitely had something 'different' about them... Well I have finally put my finger on it.

Kindness and compassion

Most leaders have something that makes them stand out from the rest. Leaders usually take a risk by doing something different from others. Have great ideas and put them into practice. A leader will spot potential in an employee who might just need a little push or encouragement. This patience and perseverance has kindness all over it. Like 'giving someone a chance'.

Most leaders started from scratch. They were the 'nerds' in school,who had to work their way to the top. Most leaders assist others to bring out their potential. I have certainly noticed this.

- Leaders are **flexible and ready for change**.
- Leaders **communicate well** and **empower their employees** to work to their best ability

➤ Leaders have **courage and patience**.

Kindness is a virtue that I think is really important and I have seen a lot of leaders with this virtue recently.

➤ Leaders are **mindful** of the effect their actions will have on others.

➤ Lead **by example**

➤ Remove or decrease judgement of others as a motivational strategy. This is a huge one!!

➤ Are great Listeners. They actually **Listen**.

➤ **Assist** others without expecting anything in return. This always comes back to them in some way anyway.

➤ **Humility** has a place also. Acting aloof or above your employees does not make a good leader.

➤ Being **responsible** and also handing out accolades when people deserve them is essential and shows kindness.

A kind leader will attract like minded employees who wish to learn and will be inspired to work towards the same common goal.

'Given all we know about the need for kind, compassionate and empathetic leaders, and the apparently increasing toxic workplace, isn't it time to value and recruit leaders that embrace and exhibit kindness and compassion?'

I took the last few lines from the above article in Psychology today.

Part 2
"Your Beginner's Guide to Twitter"

Hi, Welcome to my beginners guide to Twitter.

What is Twitter? Twitter is a social networking service that allows you to send and read text messages with 140 characters.

In **English** that means that you can make a statement or sentence and put it out there to whoever is following you. This must be under 140 letters/characters.

Twitter has grown in popularity particularly among SMEs as a marketing tool to build up relationships and target potential customers. The aim would be to build your followers. This is done by being interesting enough to attract followers in the first place. Once you are consistent with interesting stuff to share, you will gain more followers which in turn will become like a little army of marketeers for you. As if they share your tweets, more people will see them that you probably wouldn't have had contact with before that.

People tend to use **Twitter** for news consumption

In 2012, **83% of users reported seeing news on Twitter. Additionally, a bulk of users are located in urban areas**

For brands, **the best time to post on Twitter is Monday through Thursday between 1pm and 3pm.**

The worst time is **after 3pm on a Friday**

What do you need to start?

You need an email address with which you sign up.

Select a password that only you will ever know - **but that you will remember**. To make this secure try to include an alphanumeric mix with no visible logic. Click 'sign up'

The next page will ask you to select people to follow. You can start by putting Twitter names you might already know (Like me for example, type @*Tweetinggoddess* into the search box). After you have followed your first five people they will ask you to follow more. But you can skip this step if you want to get cracking!

Profile and Bio:

You want to make your profile look so interesting that people will want to click on you. You want followers as followers are your new friends! They are also your very own marketing team. They are the ones who will decide if you are interesting enough or if your content (what you say in your tweets) is good enough to retweet to your followers.

---

https://Twitter.com/pauldunphy

1st short story will be published in 2014 in a book by @*AdrianMillar* it's about @*mariankeyes*! A Social media curator. See my website! designer @*AniaWebDesign*

---

https://Twitter.com/CarolFaugh

Fan of widgets and the word #*Widget* wordpress, research, social media/anthropology. MSc. A spade is a spade @*CoderDojoWexfrd*

Sign in to Twitter

Username or email

Password

Sign in ☑ Remember me · Forgot password?

New to Twitter? Sign up now »

Already using Twitter via text message? Activate your account »

Get rid of the egg!

I recommend putting a picture of **YOU** -as it attracts people - people use Twitter so makes you look more personable. If you are a small business owner, I recommend you put your picture up also. In the new style Twitter feeds, this image can now be 400 x 400px.

If you are a company, then your logo is best. A hotel? A picture of the hotel etc..

You can put your logo or icon on the background of your profile, as well as suitable visual samples of your "product". The new style Twitter profiles allow for an image of 1500 x 500px which allows plenty of space for samples, badges from various chats etc.. Take elements from your existing branding to keep consistency across all your social media platforms.

Your Bio

This should also be interesting, tell people who you are, what you do and your likes (e.g. hobbies etc.) so you will attract like minded individuals. People buy from people so even if you are a company make it sound like you are approachable and that you are going to be tweeting interesting tweets.

For example, here is my personal account profile and Bio: (now you don't have to be as personal as I am, only put up what you are comfortable with)

There is also a section to edit your profile so you put your website link into your Bio so that when people look at your profile they can simply 'click' to go straight to your website!

https:// Twitter.com/ EcoActiveIrl

EcoActiveIreland. com #Eco #EventsOnline: Hens & Dogs, Gardener, Photographer, Also @*whatsonwicklow* WOW Suite, Web & SEO via *HowToBeThe Business.com* :) Roz

Samantha Kelly
@Tweetinggoddess FOLLOWS YOU

Mum, Founder of #irishbizparty, Presenter, Speaker, Trainer. Love to see Compassion & Courage in people. Oh and I can come out with anything after 9pm!

◯ Rosslare Harbour, Ireland
🔗 tweetinggoddess.com/home/

https:// Twitter.com/ barbarascully

Writer and talker... in the papers, on TV3 Midday & presenter of The Hen House on the wireless. Mammy, cat slave, wife & dog owner... put them in order yourself

Click on the 'profile' settings section to edit your profile

Biz uses for Twitter

- Increase **brand awareness**
- Potential customers **at your fingertips**
- **Improve SEO** bringing traffic to your website
- Gives your business **the personal touch** connecting with others
- **Promote your blog**, newsletters etc.
- You can **engage** your Twitter target audience
- Your **followers help drive sales** and recommendations
- You can measure and **increase your impact**
- You can **keep an eye** on your competitors!
- Twitter helps you **reach more customers**
- You can **respond, react & retweet instantly**
- **Connect** with like-minded businesses
- People are **more likely to purchase** from a small or medium sized enterprises after they interact with them on Twitter (72%)
- It will help you **build better and more lasting relationships**
- Your brand or service will become known as the **'Go To' place or person**
- **85% say that they feel more connected to a business when following them**

Next: **Do your first tweet!!**

Start by saying something like...
'Hi Everyone, I am new to Twitter! #Newbie'
Keep it simple and be yourself. Then continue to search for people to follow. If you like gardening for example, search for any tweets that mention *#gardening* (Go to the search box) Twitter will also suggest others to follow on the left hand side of your account. You can **refresh** these suggestions if you want to search for more.

I would then recommend a second tweet containing a brief overview of what you do, or tweet about, that you can then pin to the top of your new style Twitter profile. Be sure to include a web link or image if these are relevant to your business.

Look at what the people you follow are saying... get involved and click **'reply'** if you want to add to the conversation! Click **'retweet'** if you want to share their tweet with your own followers.

To see who has mentioned you or interactions (for example who has followed you) Click on the **Connect** button. If you click on **'Home'** this is your Twitter feed. These are the tweets of everyone you are following!

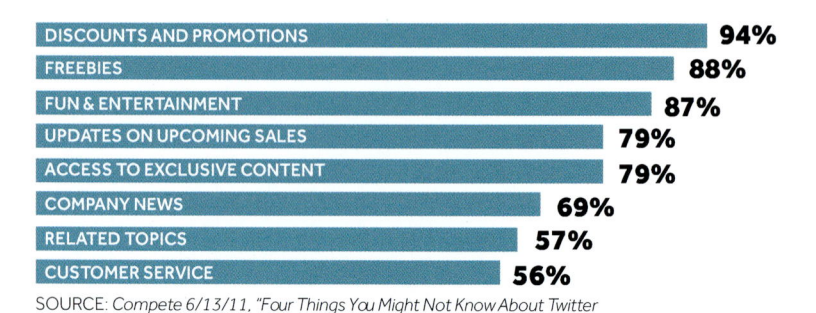

DISCOUNTS AND PROMOTIONS	94%
FREEBIES	88%
FUN & ENTERTAINMENT	87%
UPDATES ON UPCOMING SALES	79%
ACCESS TO EXCLUSIVE CONTENT	79%
COMPANY NEWS	69%
RELATED TOPICS	57%
CUSTOMER SERVICE	56%

SOURCE: *Compete 6/13/11, "Four Things You Might Not Know About Twitter*

When 140 characters are not enough

An image is worth a thousand words...

For best results, use the built in Twitter image import option (the little camera icon) to attach images to a tweet. By using this function, Twitter users will see your image directly in their feed. Instagram and other image services will only post as a link, and this removes the benefit of using an image in your post. Content supplied from Vine will also be available within the feed and adds the option of video directly within your tweet.

With the latest Twitter update, you will be able to attach up to four images to a single post, and you will also be able to tag others (up to 10 people - great for encouraging interaction).

What are the size and file type requirements for images used directly within Twitter?

➤ Your image file size can be up to 3MB.

➤ Twitter can accept GIF, JPEG, and PNG files.

➤ Twitter **WILL NOT** accept BMP, TIFF, or **animated** GIF files, due to bandwidth issues.

➤ Your photo will be automatically scaled for display in your expanded Tweet and in your user gallery.

In one study by *danzarella.com*, tweets with images uploaded to *pic.Twitter.com* were nearly **twice as likely** to be retweeted while the use of Twitpic increased the odds by just **over 60%**. On the other hand, tweets that used Facebook or Instagram links were less likely to be retweeted.

Getting deeper…

Not all messages can be effectively communicated within 140 characters nor an image. In this case, a well-phrased tweet can drive traffic from your feed to your blog where you can discuss a subject in greater depth. You can use your blog piece to link to external source information, link in a YouTube video as well as writing in more depth.

Getting personal…

If you want to tweet someone you follow Simply click on the tweet button (blue button top right) and put their Twitter name into the tweet. This is the 'Compose' tweet button. You can tweet away now.

So off you go and start tweeting! Check out my top ten tips for using Twitter effectively also!

What's new to Twitter?

Twitter is constantly being updated, but the biggest recent leap has been with images and profile page layouts.

1. More emphasis on images on profile page

Cover images are now 1500px wide giving you a greater area to display your samples, products and more.

2. Most popular/best tweets emphasised

Twitter has been redesigned to highlight tweets that get greater engagement, although there is a risk that feeds could become overtaken with cute animals, advertisers & Justin Bieber!

3. Pin Tweet

You can choose a popular or current tweet to pin to the top of your profile. Use this either to promote your USP or latest offer!

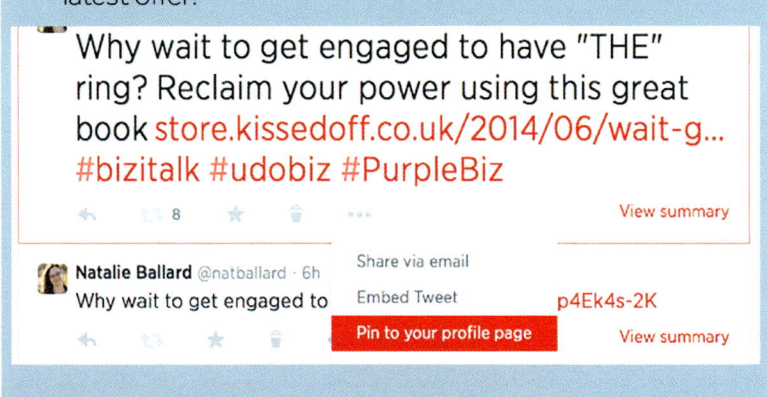

4. Filtered Tweets

Replies have their own filtered section, with photos/videos to get their own filters shortly. This update will also be ported to mobile shortly.

Tweets   Tweets and replies

 Pinned Tweet
Natalie Ballard @natballard · Apr 24

A drop of ink can make a million think! The power of the written word could be yours. kissedoff.co.uk #bizitalk #udobiz

↰ ⇄ 8 ★ 1

Twitter lingo and what it means

Top terms you must know when you start on Twitter!

- **hashtag** - A hashtag or # is used to categorize topics or subjects of interest on Twitter. For example if you are watching *#Gameofthrones* search for this hashtag and you will see all tweets that mention the program. You can join in the conversation by following the hashtag. You just say what you have to say... and then put *#Gameofthrones* (your tweet will appear in the stream)

- **RT** - This means *Retweet* - If someone says something that you think will be of interest to your followers then you can retweet it to them. (A bit like forwarding an email) If you share something valuable (or need word spread about something you can ask for a RT) although it is better to get a RT without asking.

- **FF** - *#FollowFriday* - This is a popular hashtag that you can use to recommend users to your own followers.

- **DM** - Direct message. You can send messages privately to someone who is following you!

- **Tweetup** - a 'real world' meeting of people who are on Twitter. (I highly recommend these tweet ups! It is so much fun putting a face to a name in the virtual world. They are almost always the way you expect them to be. (This goes for idiots and bores on Twitter also though)! You will probably find that you aren't following them... can make for awkward conversations.

- **Twitterati** - Celebrity tweeters or well known A list tweeters.

- **Peeps/Tweeps** - people on Twitter!

- **Lurker** - Someone who is always reading tweets and keeping an eye on things but doesn't tweet much themselves. I have met lots of them! They seem to know everything that is going on, but don't like to get involved (or sometimes they are just shy).

What else?

You are on Twitter and you see the top trends on the left hand side. What does this mean?

> **2/3 of Twitter users are under 35**

Well, these topics are the most popular topics right now on Twitter! By including one of these hashtags (so long as it is relevant to your message) you can reach beyond your existing followers.

For trending topics you will usually find out about big events that are going on in the world or active discussions. Click on them to see.

You can change the location on trending topics. Mine are set to 'Ireland' as you can see. But if you want to see what is the most popular in Brazil you can do that or just see worldwide trends. Just click on 'Change'

WHO DO I FOLLOW - WHAT DOES IT MEAN WHEN I FOLLOW SOMEONE?

A follower is someone that follows you on Twitter. This does not mean you have to follow them back - a person can follow you without you following them. However, it's best if you follow your followers back, this way you can both engage with one another. People like to know that you are interested in what they have to tweet about.

If someone is annoying you, Just 'Unfollow' or if they are being abusive 'block' them. (Just click on their profile, see where it says 'following' arrow down and you will see 'block'.

unfollowers.me is a great tool for keeping track of your followers, unfollowers and fake followers. If you find people unfollowing you whose content is not relevant to you, then unfollow. Unfollows are not shown in Twitter and not highlighted to the individual you have unfollower unless they use a third party service.

Irish Twitter Trends

Discovery, the new planning and insights unit of Havas owned *eightytwenty*, have conducted extensive research into how Twitter is being used in Ireland. The key findings of the study indicate;

- As little as 160 tweets could get you trending
- Sports and Politics are the most popular topics
- Wednesday is the busiest day on Twitter
- 10pm to 11pm is the busiest hour each day
- Dublin & Cork users post almost half of all Irish tweets

See more at: *http://www.eightytwenty.ie/blog/how-Twitter-is-used-in-ireland/#sthash.IMdjaFPP.dpuf*

As you might know, I always start my workshops with your **Twitter Bio**. Your Bio on Twitter is the most important part of starting your journey into Twitter. We must find the Bio interesting so the secret to more followers is to make your Bio stand out.

Ask yourself... is it interesting enough? Is it positive enough? Can you read it properly? Why should I follow you? What makes you stand out from everyone else? Where are you located? These questions are very important especially if you are a Business Twitter account.

Us Tweeters are an impatient bunch. We make a split second decision on whether we want to follow you or not. We look at what your profile says and see if we might find you interesting enough to interact and engage with you.

80% of UK Tweeters access Twitter on their mobiles!

"Your Beginner's Guide to Twitter"

So here are the list of reasons why I won't follow you.

1. **You have no photo up.**
   Please don't be an 'Egghead' I don't trust you straight away and also think you are lazy for not putting a picture up. I can't understand it. You might be saying something interesting but really I won't click 'Follow' as I really don't trust you. OK, if you are shy or hate yourself in pictures, put up your logo or a flower, your dog, the sea... anything that is part of you.

2. **No description** of who you are and your interests or a description of your business if you are a business. I won't click 'Follow' to just anyone. They need to have a description that will make me want to engage with you. For example, I love certain characteristics such as dignity, compassion and courage. So hopefully I will attract like-minded positive folk. I am also a Mum and there is a description of awards and what I do there. Think about it... Who do you want to attract? I see some wonderful, funny Bios which instantly tell me these people are going to be great fun to follow! I like the quirkiness of it and the fact that they made the effort to stand out!
   No Website If you are a business, I want to know how I can order your product. So a website or Facebook/LinkedIn link or even a contact number is essential. No point in promoting what you do if I can't get in touch with you!

3. **Negative Bio** - Ones that describe or put people down in the Bio or are bitchy. Yes these guys exist (and don't really have many followers). I also look at the most recent tweets and if they aren't positive or at least interesting then I am not going to follow them.

4. **Sexy Bio** - not many of them around, usually are spammers but even ones with a guy showing off his six pack just don't interest me. From experience they are usually married and will start Direct Messaging you with all sorts of proposals.

5. **Nothing in common** I get the strangest followers sometimes who are into all sorts which I really have no idea why they followed me as we have nothing in common. They don't get a follow back!

Who do I follow?

Interesting folk, Good people, funny people, Entrepreneurs especially start ups (We all need to assist one another so I always like to see if there is any way I can assist). SMEs, Women in business, People promoting health etc.. (hoping I will learn something), foodies and nice restaurants and hotels. Also inspirational leaders. The list goes on. But you can bet that they don't have any of the 5 previous points on their profile!

#Hashtags

I teach Twitter workshops and perhaps the most common question I get asked has to be 'What is a hashtag anyway?' So I decided to do a little blog all about hashtags and what they are for. Blogs are a great way for dealing with any FAQs you get asked on social media platforms as no one wants to hear the same answer over and over again!

A hashtag is a word or phrase preceded by a **# symbol** (Option + 3 on a Mac) to identify a particular topic or popular event that is taking place. E.g. If you see *#Liverpool* chances are there is a tweet chat going on about Liverpool or a big game on that folk are tweeting about.

The most popular hashtag was Hibernian Training as we were holding a competition on *#irishbizparty* that night. But see that if you click on *#Juniorcert* most likely this was because the Junior Cert results were out the next day and people were chatting about this.

So, if you wanted to tweet about the Late late show, you would include *#Latelate* in your tweet to join the conversation. Click on a hashtag to see all the posts that mention the subject in real time

How can hashtags help me in business?

Use relevant hashtags to your business:
See what hashtags other businesses in your field are using. You can search for relevant hashtags to your business. For example if you are in the beauty trade, put *#Beauty* in the search box. If your target market is Mums put *#Mums* in the search box. See what comes up, every Tweeter who has used the hashtag *#Mums*. This way you can see others in the business, or see their followers, keep an eye on possible competitors etc..

If you're promoting a wedding product I would use *#Bridal #Wedding #Bride* for example. I bet if you put *#Bridal* in the search box you will find lots of others who are in your industry. You should follow some of these users and they could become allies especially if you are doing wedding stationery and they are doing gowns!

There are popular hashtags used by businesses also. For example **#Weddinghour** is on from 9-10pm and is very popular with all bridal and wedding suppliers. Follow **@Weddinghour** for more info.

Some hashtags will also automatically RT to a particular group of followers, and you will learn to pick up the ones that do this very quickly. A great way of getting an offer out to a large number of people with little time spent on your part. You can combine hashtags to reach an even greater audience also.

Daily hashtags in use which help promote Business

#FPSBS *@Teamfreddiepig*

#Purplebiz *@Purpledognet* - The more you RT #purplebiz tweets the higher up their rankings you get and the more RTs you get.

#Bizitalk *@Bizitalk* - This is a great way to spread the word to millions of people, and as a paid member you get a lot of sponsored tweets that are automatically scheduled.

#udobiz *@udotweet* - Similar to @Bizitalk, U-Do is another social enterprise style setup which is just moving into area affiliates. "Join U-Do. Promote your business offers, blogs, events & more. Connect with potential customers. Make trusted contacts & friends. Grow your business Have fun."

#Womaninbiz #Wineoclock *@AwardingWomen* - *#Womaninbiz* is both a daily retweet hashtag as well as a popular chat hour.

Weekly hashtags & Tweet chats

There are a variety of Twitter chats - based on geographical location, business sector, interests and more. Here are a selection of my favourites.

#Irishbizparty - *@irishbizparty* - Every Wednesday night from 9-11pm GMT .for small business owners in Ireland who want to promote what they do and meet others just like them! A **#Starbiz** is selected each week also. The Starbiz gets to host the hashtag the following week! They also win a mug from *@Clubcolours_ie*

#Brtishbizparty - Mondays 9-10pm GMT Networking in your pjs... for small business owners in the UK who want to promote what they do and meet others just like them!

#Galwayhour - Tuesday nights 9pm-11pm

#Twittersisters - Every Thursday 8.30 -9.30 pm

There are also a lot of regional and town based chats that connect businesses with charities and other local bodies.

Competitions

Twitter competitions are great for business - whether you are running them or taking part!

@Theopaphitis #SBS - Between 5 -7.30 Every Sunday evening. Theo retweets his favourite 6 entries! Just tweet what you do using *@Theopaphitis* and put *#SBS* in the tweet!

@Jacqueline_gold #Wow - Between 1pm and 3pm every Wednesday just tweet using Jacqueline's name and the hashtag *#WOW* - She will choose her favourite 3 businesses!

There are lots and lots of others! So if you see a hashtag being used in a tweet, click on it and check it out. There are lots of funny ones that go around too, so keep an eye out and join in!

"Your Beginner's Guide to Twitter"

Timetable

Monday

1-2pm
#EcomChat
E-Commerce

8-9pm Peak slot for regional hours

9-10pm
#BritishBizParty
UK wide chat

Tuesday

8-9pm Peak slot for regional hours

Wednesday

8-9pm Peak slot for regional hours

9-11pm
#IrishBizParty
Irish biz chat

Thursday

8-9pm Peak slot for regional hours

Friday

3-4pm *#GBHour*
UK wide biz chat

Saturday

9-10am
#satchatuk
UK wide chat

I am amazed at the amount of businesses here in Ireland who have yet to join Twitter. Not only that, I am even more amazed at how many aren't actually using the Twitter account that they already have set up!

I have often asked Twitter for recommendations for hotels for when I go to a different city on business. I always get recommendations back with the hotel name so the hotel can see that they are being recommended and then respond quickly to get me as a customer. But on one occasion only one hotel out of the 5 responded.

People online want a fast response. If you have a Twitter presence that is active, you won't miss anything like this. If however, you created an account and just tweet whenever something big is coming up like a concert or match, it isn't enough.

There was a recent study done on Twitter use in Ireland. It found that users are:

- Mostly active in Dublin and Cork
- Key spots of high activity exist's outside of the capital in Louth, Meath, Kildare, Wicklow and Waterford
- A high proportion of users are aged 15 – 35
- Most activity occurs in the first half of the week
- Users are active from midday onwards
- The busiest time on Twitter is from 8pm to 11pm

Source: Eightytwenty *http://www.eightytwenty.ie/blog/how-Twitter-is-used-in-ireland/*

So... what time are you tweeting? Are you hitting these times? Are you targeting these potential customers? Even if they aren't your target market, they have parents, sisters, brothers etc. who might need a birthday gift etc.. So they are still **potential customers and your very own army of marketeers and advertisers**.

For me, as a Twitter user, I always keep an eye out for deals and gift ideas that I can perhaps use later. I often 'Favourite' interesting items and articles that I can look back on later. So even if they don't order or book now, the fact that they saw your brand and it is visible means that it will stick in their heads for when they DO need your service or product.

You don't just create a Twitter account and leave it there. To me as a follower of your account, it makes me feel 'Well I followed you, which means you have a potential ally here. So you could at least **interact** and acknowledge my existence?' I don't want to see constant 'ads' and statements, I want you to engage with me.

Value me as a **Follower** and **Retweet my tweets** from time to time also if I say something that might relate to your industry especially.

Having a Twitter presence can mean the difference between someone booking or ordering from you! For example - If I am out with the girls and we are discussing going away together I can say 'Hang on they are on Twitter, I will ask them'... you reply and you've most likely got a booking right there!

Things move fast on Social Media, people now have Twitter on their phones. An instant connection to you and your business. Don't waste it! Get your Twitter presence active and engage with your customers before someone else does!

What is the favourite button for on Twitter? Well, some people say it's to mark something that you want to read later on. So if you are really busy and just skimming through your Twitter feed, you can mark tweets you think look interesting and read back later when you have more time.

But lately I have seen a few discussions about this button on Twitter. Some people think it is being misused as a way of getting your attention. If I see someone has 'Favourited' my tweet, I check their Bio to see who they are if I don't know them. Is it a way to get my attention in the hope that I will follow? Or is it just a way of letting me know that, "Yes I have read your tweet, it got my attention, but I won't be retweeting it for you or reading it right now." Which is fair enough. But rarely do I see a late RT or comment afterwards. Do 'favourited' tweets get lost somewhere?

Those tweets you do favourite however now have a dedicated space on your profile page...

Do we check the tweets that we have clicked 'Favourite' on.

Do you know how to check your favourites? Well, if you go to the 'sun' symbol between the message symbol and the 'compose tweet' symbol… go to 'lists'. On the left hand side you should see 'Favourites'… click on this and you will see all the tweets you have Favourited.

On the new Twitter profiles, favourites become much more visible. Since the favourites list is a prominent link on your profile now, make sure that the tweets you've favourited are tweets you don't mind your followers seeing if they poke around your profile page.

I think it would be great if Twitter had an extra button that said **'Interesting'** as I think the Favourite button is used for this also. A bit similar to the 'like' button on Facebook! There are many times someone clicks 'favourite' and then retweets the tweet immediately. (Thanks)

So are we treating it as a highlighter? A like button? Or are we all using it correctly to list tweets that we like and want to read later?

A good way of using the 'Favourite' button is to gather positive feedback on your account. If you have a list of positive feedback (favourites) then not only does this make you look like you are doing a good job (if you are having a bad day, just look through all your favourites lol) but it also shows the person who tweeted that you have seen this tweet and are acknowledging them. So it is a kind of interaction. So everyone feels good.

You can spot them a mile away! The popular and active Twitter users. Their names pop up even at times when you don't expect them to! But just seeing their name and brand for even a split second keeps them in your sub conscious so that when you go searching for interesting stuff on Twitter, you know you can rely on them to be either having a debate about something or being funny or they will have some really interesting content to share. That's why you are following them yes?

Well good Twitter users have good habits… Here are some:

They are **consistent**. Most of the time the topic they tweet about is what they specialise in. Let's face it if a restaurant started tweeting about beauty it might scare you away! You followed them in the first place because of the subject they tweet about. Or perhaps you noticed that they share funny stories etc.. So you don't want them going all serious and down in the dumps either.

They are also full of useful **information**. Whether it is the latest news or the latest trick or tip, they are knowledgeable and mix it up a bit so you are kept interested.

They are usually very **helpful**. They know how important it is to engage and build relationships… I am sure if you look back on their tweets you will see that they RT a lot and give helpful advice or tips.

They usually **respond** to tweets within 24 hours.

They **Tweet** a lot! Expect impromptu pics of a flower or tree or sunset… anything that they think you will appreciate they will take a pic and tweet it out, so they have their Twitter on their smartphone for sure!

Expect plenty of **interaction and engagement** from Top Tweeters. They are almost always chatting to someone and usually involved in something interesting that is going on at the time!

Popular hashtags will lead you to find some great tweeters. Try the *#Latelate* hashtag and the *#Vinb* one if you like politics. And to find lots of nice friendly entrepreneurs try *#irishbizparty, #Twittersisters, #sbs*.

So create some good habits on Twitter and you could become one of those Top Tweeters yourself! Off you go now!

I had a lovely day today… the sun was shining and people were out and about walking dogs and in their gardens checking out the state of them after the storms and Winter neglect. Well, I was anyway! I took the 7 year old and my dogs for a walk to the shops, a simple trip that really made me happy. Kids just want your company and time most of the time.

As an avid Twitter user I have tried to find a balance between how long I spend on it recently. Of course what I do means I am on it all week from 8- 3.15 when my Daughter comes home from school. But now I turn it off, do her homework, make the dinner, light the fire and do some kind of activity with both children in the evenings. But for me when they go to bed is when Twitter comes alive. I think I am not alone as the most popular time to Tweet is between 10 and 11pm.

I have made a lot of friends on Twitter who I have also met in real life. I've made connections with people in different countries who I haven't met yet, but we have so much in common. I am sure I will meet them someday as most of them are Entrepreneurs like myself. Someday I am sure I will be travelling further afield to do workshops and speaking moments or networking at big events.

Anything is possible! I have learned over the years on Twitter, who are the funny Tweeters, who make me smile, who are the big softies who make me feel nice. Who are the ones who care about animals, the environment, politics, health etc.. I surround myself with people like this in my life offline so on Twitter I seek out people like this also.

My Bio says I love 'Courage, Dignity and Compassion' So I will probably attract like minded people. This is how I end up chatting with the type of folk I would like to hang out with. You have all got to know me through my honesty and mood swings, my struggles, my financial worries, my battle with the cigarettes and my yearning to be a size ten. You have kept me going, encouraged me to stop smoking, encouraged me to try new things.

A little comment here, a funny picture or saying there… it all helps me to keep at it, keep coming back to see you all. Some don't understand it all… think I'm a bit mad… but you know what? I'd rather be hanging out with most of you guys who I know understand me than the people who say they can't understand it. I have real friends outside of Twitter who understand me too. They make me feel good, make me smile, encourage me and are positive people.

So I ain't going nowhere… Twitter keeps me sane and makes me smile. If I am feeling lonely I know that I can log on and there will be someone there to chat to me. So that is good enough for me.

You will get to know which groups will be where, the more you interact and tweet. I do most of my tweeting in the evenings because to be honest I don't have much of a social life as I am separated with two children, so Twitter is now my social life! But I can honestly say that 4 of my best friends I actually met on Twitter!! So if you see *#Tweetups* being advertised, do go along to them. (These are meet ups for people on Twitter so you actually get to meet the people you are tweeting with)

All of these tips are just how I use Twitter. I am sure there are many more formal ways, but this is just how I use it. The most important things for me are interact, interact, interact and engage, engage, engage!!

No one is going to be interested in what you have got to say, if you aren't interested in them! Be genuine also, People can sense when someone is a bit false or insincere and prefer honesty. I tend to mix my business tweets with some personal stuff that is going on, and I also use humour a lot.

So what are you waiting for? There is a whole new world on Twitter waiting to meet you!

Sometimes we need a little reminder of how different we are in how we think and do things. It ain't easy, taking the risk of setting up a business from an idea and bringing it to market. We learn as we go, put our own money and all our energy into our 'baby'.

Twitter tips

Twitter has really changed my life... before Twitter I was lonely, felt unconnected and had lost a lot of confidence. But one day when my sister introduced me to Twitter because I had a business, I embraced this new world and started to make new friends from all over the world. I became really good at it, took to it like a duck to water! And so now I have put together some tips just for you.

1. When you create your account, your username should be similar to your brand e.g. I am @*Tweetinggoddess* on Twitter and that is the name of my business! That way, every time you tweet something, your brand is also coming up!

2. Start by following people who would be interested in what you do! For example, if you are a chef and blog about food, follow people who love to cook, or who write about food! Journalists are always good ones to follow I find. Or check out *#foodies* (the hashtag highlights groups or popular topics on Twitter at the moment so always check your 'trending' subjects and see what is popular today!)

3. Also, follow people or friends who you know are already on Twitter and who have a reputation for retweeting or supporting the work that you are doing.

4. Tweet interesting tweets, If it is a beautiful morning where you are, say it!! If you come across as positive, people will gravitate towards you. Tweet about what you do e.g. if you are a chef say something like *'We are looking forward to cooking our new prawn special today, juicy prawns so fresh from the market!'* Get people's attention.

5. Tweet about some personal stuff too, like if your daughter loses her tooth, say that you have the tooth fairy coming! I guarantee you will get replies to that one, because others can identify with it. If there is something in the news, comment on it

6. Read the tweets of those who you are following and if you see something that you feel your own followers would like, then Retweet it! The person who put the tweet up will instantly get a notification that you have done this, so you are already getting attention from them and they will most likely RT you when you need one.

7. When commenting on things that are in the news, don't get too controversial. You want to attract positive people who will support you not start arguing with you! Also if people are challenging you, this will be noticed by others and your brand will be associated with arguing... even if you are right, just stop commenting and leave the conversation.

8. If you wish to comment on something or say things a little more personal, use the DM or direct message section. This way only you or the other person will see it.

9. Interact, Interact, Interact... for example, if you see someone is having a bad day, ask them about it, or just simply say. 'Aw sorry to hear you are having a hard time, sending you a hug' or something like that. (OK Lads, I know you won't be saying that but something similar would be something like 'hang in there' or 'tomorrow is a new day). This makes the person feel like you care and makes them feel less lonely and understood. Believe me, there are a lot of people out there that just want to be heard.

10. Tweet!!! It is as simple as that!! I tweet in the morning and at lunchtime, then in the afternoons I check in to see what is happening... There are lots of Mums on Twitter in the mornings I've noticed and a very active group on Twitter in the evenings so I tweet a lot when the kids go to bed.

Twitter Rules:

- You may not impersonate others
- Do not claim usernames on behalf of businesses
- Do not publish or post other people's private information
- Do not publish or post direct, specific threats of violence
- Comply with Copyright procedures

Ad Policies updated March 2014

1. Keep users safe.
2. Promote honest content and target it responsibly.
3. Don't distribute spam, harmful code, or other disruptive content.
4. Set high editorial standards for the Twitter Ads content you create.
5. Set high standards for the off-Twitter connections you create.
6. Be informed about the Twitter Ads processes

Twitter restricts (but not bans) the promotion of products or services in the following categories:

- Alcohol content
- Financial services
- Gambling content
- Health and pharmaceutical products and services
- Political campaigning

TWITTER CARDS

What are they?

Image courtesy of www.webtrends.com

How do they work?

When enabled, there is an option to 'view summary', click and the image or media appears.

Are they beneficial to my business?

YES. WHY?

➤ Your name stays on the retweet even if your retweeter doesn't tag you.

➤ Results in more followers.

➤ Needn't keep tweets short (for RTs)

➤ One click follow button at bottom of card

➤ Can display author name as well as publisher website

How do I set them up?

➤ Ask your webmaster to hard code it for you on your website,

➤ or, use Wordpress plugin **Yoast SEO**
click on *social>Twitter* and click *card validator* to apply
Once the application is made, it takes Twitter a few weeks to approve it.

Twitter Advertising

See: *https://support.twitter.com/articles/20169693-Twitter-ads-policies*

There are 3 main types of Twitter ads

1. **Promoted Tweets:** Drive an Action e.g.. sign-up, sale, other promotion or photo
2. **Promoted Account:** Brand awareness, increase followers
3. **Promoted Trends:** Time sensitive, Events, TV etc..

Can be highly targeted! Gender, geography, language etc..

Part 3
Moving Forward

What is an Entrepreneur anyway? The definition I most identify with is this one:

'An Entrepreneur is a person who sets up a business or businesses, taking on financial risks in the hope of profit.'

I have put together some quotes that I find very inspiring and can identify with!

DON'T BE AFRAID TO FAIL

BE AFRAID TO NOT TRY

"It's not about ideas. It's about making ideas happen."
- Scott Belsky, Behance co-founder

"The way to get started is to quit talking and begin doing."
- Walt Disney, Disney founder

"Trust your instincts."
- Estee Lauder, Estee Lauder founder

"Don't worry about people stealing your design work. Worry about the day they stop."
- Jeffrey Zeldman, A List Apart publisher

"I have not failed. I've just found 10,000 ways that won't work".
- Thomas Edison

"I don't know the key to success, but the key to failure is trying to please everybody."
- Bill Cosby

"Success is not the key to happiness. Happiness is the key to success. If you love what you are doing, you will be successful."
- Albert Schweitzer

Successful people are always looking for opportunities to help others. Unsuccessful people are asking, What's in it for me?
- Brian Tracy

More reading: Five qualities of successful Entrepreneurs:
http://www.entrepreneur.com/article/227776

I have met many wonderful entrepreneurs on my journey through the Roller coaster of being in business. My own story has been one of many struggles, including the usual ones of having no money to get things moving, driving around with the petrol gauge on 'E' and paying myself last!

But I am finding out more and more through running *#irishbizparty* that there are people out there who are working really hard instead of claiming social welfare and really trying to make something of themselves. They aren't getting help from Enterprise boards etc.., as they aren't 'Exporting' for example. Also, there are lots of things coming up to help start ups… what about the businesses who are already running a few years. Don't they deserve help too?

I started *#irishbizparty* as a hashtag just to have some fun really and meet others like me but now it has turned into a really positive support network.

More info *https://www.youtube.com/watch?v=PjDko9n91eA&feature=youtu.be*

I often get calls from people who take part, and meet others for a cuppa just to chat. It is important just to listen sometimes… I know for me, having someone to talk to made a big difference.

Sometimes when you have a business you can only see one side of it. Your side. This is our baby and we are very protective of it. We think we know everything there is to know about it and indeed we are probably right. But sometimes it is good to get someone who isn't so involved in what we do to look at it from another angle.

For example:

What do you do exactly? You might know what you do and be an expert in it… but do others actually listen and understand what you do?

Are you trying out other social networks… perhaps Twitter isn't the right platform for you? Perhaps Pinterest is better… if your target market is teens, they are not on Facebook as much as before for example. They are on Snapchat amongst others.

Is yours a business that relies on referrals from customers? Are you asking your customers for testimonials? Are you getting out and meeting people who might be able to help you spread the word?

I have found that there is a gap in the whole networking thing. There seems to be a real fear of attending networking events. The whole 'fake it till you make it' thing I really don't agree with. For me honesty works much better.

So what if you can't buy oil and barely have enough petrol to attend these events. Am not going to pretend I am loaded and put on an act. Why should I? Take me as I am. Hard working, kind, willing to help where I can, outgoing, bit mad and funny.

There is a new breed of Entrepreneurs out there right now, especially on irishbizparty who are honest, share their knowledge with each other, collaborate and refer business to each other. I have witnessed it many times and have met some wonderful people through *#irishbizparty*. We are delighted that Independent.ie have linked up with us also thanks to Ailish O Hora …they can see the positivity that is being created here.

So be part of it… let's get this country back on it's feet… let's assist one another and make sure that we all get something out of it. We don't need to step on others to get what we want. This is totally unnecessary. If you assist others, it will come back to you.

(If you want to be part of the *#irishbizparty* website email *Aidan@avalanchedesigns.ie*. Thank you to Independent.ie who feature the *#Starbiz* we select every Wednesday on *#irishbizparty* …this is a huge emotional boost for a small business owner and a great platform for them to show what they do. So join in the hashtag *#irishbizparty* every Wednesday from 9-11pm. See you there)!

We also have *#Britishbizparty* now on Monday nights from 9-10pm!

How to get sales from Twitter

Twitter is great for building relationships and making new connections. But how do you turn them into sales?

Its so important to make sure you get as much info into a tweet as you can. Ask yourself

- Is the tweet **interesting** to the reader?
- Is it worth a **Retweet**?
- **Why** would I retweet it?
- Is the **timing** of the tweet good? For example is it a food item? Tweet before lunch or dinner.
- Is it a glamorous dress item? Are women **online** now? Is there talk about an upcoming event or wedding? Celebrity wedding perhaps?
- Have you included a **photo**?
- Is there a 'call to action' that is… a link to the item you want to sell with a **'buy now'** option? Us tweeters are very lazy when it comes to looking for stuff, we want to see it now and just 'click'

So…

1. Does your tweet have interesting eye catching statement?
2. Picture
3. Link to buy.
4. Does your tweet tell the reader what you want them to do?
5. Include a hashtag to improve your reach (e.g. wedding service… put *#weddinghour #Brides*). You don't have to put # at the end of the Tweet.
6. Is your personality in the Tweet?
7. Use shortened URLs (links… try *Bitly.com*)

Here is an example of a tweet that has a bit of everything. Includes fun, call to action with link to book and a photo. Also hashtags that are popular.

Whites of Wexford
@WhitesofWexford

Apr 24

Anyone need a bit of this? Book online *http://bit.ly/Pu7uKf pic.Twitter.com/oMvlI5bH3q"* *#Spa #Travel #Wexford*

However, I wouldn't do too many of these. I always say the perfect way to get more sales from Twitter is to build **relationships** first… your followers are your own army of marketeers so build relationships first then when you have something to promote they will RT or share for you automatically as they like you and like what you do.

So if you have made a really great connection on Twitter and you chat a lot I would move the relationship offline. Suggest you meet for a cuppa someday when you are in their area.

This way you are nurturing the relationship. When you meet face to face it brings it to a whole new level. Both of you will know instinctively when someone asks for someone for a particular service you will stick in each others heads.

This means recommendations… which means leads… which turn to sales!

I met Debbie from **Decadent Beauty** on Twitter and now she does my make up every time I have a big event!! On Wednesday I recommended her to other ladies and they got theirs done too! **David Mc Auley** took this picture!! Oh and by the way I met him on Twitter too!

Part 4
Twitter Stories

Your Network is your Net worth

Below is a photo of Bill Liao and I. We met through Twitter and he has assisted me a lot on my journey. We both have teenage daughters with type 1 diabetes so this was how our conversation initially started. He has been very kind with his time and has the patience of a saint! Sometimes I need to reeled in a bit and he is very good at that. I have made many wonderful connections through Bill and his network. And vice versa. Using your network and giving some of your time freely to those who need is a lovely thing to do and I know Bill does this for others. It has taught me that these things really do come back to you in different ways. Perhaps not in monetary terms but definitely in other ways such as feeling good about it and enhancing another's life can actually enhance yours!

I always try to be helpful especially to start ups and like to promote assisting one another as much as I can. Just a coffee with someone can make all the difference to them if they are struggling. So this is just a little thank you for Bill.

> **During your time on Twitter, you will find stories happening to you! This is a selection of mine.**

Tony Ennis

I met Tony Ennis of Ennis & Co. Business Consultants 5 years ago when he was delivering a Wexford County Enterprise Board Start your own business course in Wexford. He was so full of energy and so warm and friendly I couldn't believe this guy was for real to be honest. But he is! When I got my idea for Funky Goddess he was the first person I rang. He was so kind and gave his time freely and we met and chatted about my plan. He was so supportive and even though I was constantly calling into his office and sometimes bursting into tears even, he was always patient and listened and then got straight to the point of what I needed to do next.

Tony has mentored me all along my journey and has been at the end of the phone with advice and I am so grateful for his support and valuable tips and insights. Thank you Tony, none of this would have been possible without your support and friendship.

Good Twitter Use

Good Twitter use....House hotel Galway

SarahHamiltonMakeup @SarahHMakeup

Hello **#irishbizparty** Anyone know of a venue for a fashion photoshoot for Sunday in the Limk/Clare/Galway region? Had a last min let down :(

BridalBroochBouquet @kaysschool

@SarahHMakeup @Tweetinggoddess most hotels will let you use them, they are usually glad to get featured

Samantha Kelly @Tweetinggoddess

@kaysschool @SarahHMakeup I think the @The_House_Hotel would be lovely

House Hotel @The_House_Hotel

@Tweetinggoddess @kaysschool @SarahHMakeup Would be delighted to have you! I'm in tomorrow if you'd like to call, Aislinn x 091538900

THE PUNCTURE

I had to write this article as a huge Thank you and to show the power of Twitter and how assisting others can come back to you in a way you would never expect!

Myself and the other half decided to take the kids to Huntington Castle which is about an hour and half drive from where I live. We had a fab day with lovely weather and the kids were happy! Yay!

On the way back home however, we got a puncture. My other half had been meaning to get a new wheel brace for a while but kept forgetting to do it. Well… was he stressed or what when he realised he couldn't get the nuts off with the one he had!

We were on the M9, an extremely busy motorway, and because we were on the hard shoulder, we got the kids out of the car and on to the bank for safety.

I had some battery left on my phone so I put a tweet out (Just to see what would happen)

'Please help, we have a puncture and are on the road 5 miles sth of Athy battery low' and gave my other half's number.

Now my other half was very stressed and thought I was a right eejit! He said 'yeah whatever, there's no way someone is going to help us from Twitter!'

JOE TO THE RESCUE!

Well would you believe it? After a few retweets Joe came on Twitter asking whereabouts we were. It turns out he was sitting in his car eating his chicken curry before he headed home and was checking his tweets!!

So he rang the number and said he was on his way! Now let me tell you about Joe. Joe has a daughter who has Rett syndrome and he does a lot of charity fundraising etc. to raise awareness for Nathalia. So anytime I saw a tweet from him, I would Retweet it to others for him. He is also an Entrepreneur here in Ireland and runs a security company

http://www.safewatchsecurity.ie/

Also, Joe always retweets articles he finds interesting.

JOE CAME ALONG AND HAD THE WHEEL BRACE ETC., HELPED US ALL HE COULD UNTIL THE ROADSIDE ASSISTANCE ARRIVED.

We greeted each other with a hug as we had never met, yet had been friends on Twitter for about a year! My other half was baffled as he just doesn't get Twitter at all

It is Entrepreneurs like Joe who work hard, have their own day to day issues, yet still have time to assist others. A perfect example of a good person doing his best and the type of connection I love to make!

THANK YOU JOE LAWLOR!

Connect with Joe on Twitter!
https://twitter.com/JoeLawlor1

Oh and Joe's curry chips went cold because he was busy assisting us! Sorry about that Joe! Thank you so much Twitter.

The Justin Bieber Ticket!

I use social media a lot as you may know. I have a 13 year old daughter who was very upset as we couldn't get her tickets to Justin Bieber's concert in Dublin. She was crying in her room and I decided... right!! Let's try Twitter and see if we can get a ticket.

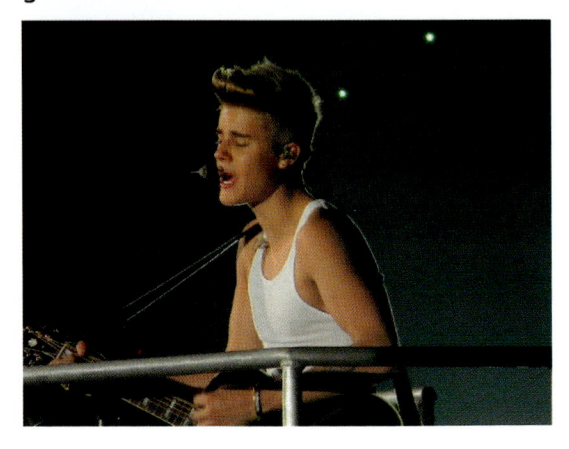

So I put a tweet out asking did anyone have a spare ticket on Twitter and Facebook. Got lots of RTs from people and folks were really nice spreading the word for me. That Tweet reached thousands of timelines.

HOW ONE BUSINESS HELPED ME

I used to run a company called Funky Goddess which produced gift boxes for girls approaching the awkward milestone of a first period. When I shelved it, I referred customers to a competitor who I like called 'My Secrets'.

So because I have been helpful to Ann and My Secrets, Ann was more than happy to assist by putting the request for a ticket up on her Facebook page. A lady contacted her that had a spare ticket!!

So I rang Sinead (The lady with the ticket) and we chatted for a long time and arranged to meet outside the O2. When we met and I could see that she was normal lol, they went into the concert with her niece (who was most importantly also a belieber) and she had a ball!!

MORAL OF THE STORY?

Always keep connections even if they are competitors as you just never know how you can assist each other in the future

Always use social media to make new connections.

When you assist others it always comes back to you!

NOW I JUST HAVE TO LISTEN TO JUSTIN BIEBER FOR THE FORESEEABLE FUTURE ..IN THE CAR…ON THE CD PLAYER ETC.

Twitter Xmas story

by Noel Cuddy
https://Twitter.com/noelcuddy

Have to tell you this true story of what happened 2 years ago when I was relatively new to Twitter. I had gone to a couple of tweet ups and met a few of my followers and some new friends. One of them was Noel Cuddy. We often tweeted back and forth and he was great at guiding me especially with tips for business etc..

Christmas was approaching and my then 5 year old decided at the last minute that she wanted a 'Jessie' doll from Toy Story. Abi is hearing impaired and has a severe language delay so I really wanted to make Xmas special for her as she has had to go to speech therapy every week and she was at that stage when she was starting to realise she was a bit different from her friends. I searched all the toy shops here in Wexford but alas, they were all sold out.

So in desperation I put up a Tweet asking if anyone had seen 'Jessie' dolls on their shopping travels. I received a tweet from Noel saying that he was in a Toy store in Swords and he was 'looking at the doll right now!' He asked did I want him to get it and then somehow get it down to me. I couldn't believe it.

So… as I live in Wexford and he lives near the airport, I contacted a man I knew who drove the Wexford Bus from the airport to Wexford and asked him would it be OK if Noel gave him the doll to bring to Wexford!! He said no problem, so I gave him the money, Noel met the bus at the airport and I got a tweet saying:

'Jessie is on the bus!'

Thank you so much Noel Cuddy (You can follow Noel here *https://Twitter.com/noelcuddy* and Wexford bus *https://Twitter.com/Wexfordbus*

We still have Jessie and Abi loves playing with her! Merry Xmas xxx

Twitter story by Bill Liao

How do you organize a scale free network of inspiring chaos?

Most organizations are about command and control and follow a pretty strict hierarchy and most organizational tools are designed with that in mind.

So what do you do when you have a network of people that need to stay in touch in a looser way? Where there is not central command and where the hierarchy is flat?

CoderDojo, the global network of clubs for kids to learn to code for free, started to using Twitter as an informal way to spread the word about what was happening in and between the clubs world wide.

While not every club has a Twitter account, most do and that has proved to be a positive boon for spreading new tips and techniques as well as sharing wonderful success stories of kids achievements.

The benefits don't stop there as the traffic on Twitter also assist in the formation of new CoderDojo's

Hundreds of clubs have sprung up all over the world where kids as young as five continue to learn cutting edge computer programming for free.

If you follow *@Liaonet's* informal list of CoderDojos for any time at all you cannot help but be inspired by what the kids are cooking up every day and by the generosity of the volunteers who make CoderDojo happen every week.

https://Twitter.com/liaonet/lists/coderdojos

LilliWhiteRose

After my daughter (AKA Lillibug) arrived and gave up work to be with her I didn't really have anything for myself to do, so my husband kept telling me to set up a blog and write about parenting. It took him a year to convince me, but then one sleepless night I decided to cave in and be productive which resulted in the setting up of my blog - LilliWhiteRose.

It is a mix of beauty reviews, some parenting stories and other ramblings. Never in a million years did I think anyone would read my blog but quickly the support of other Irish Beauty Bloggers on Twitter gave me a shot in the arm of confidence and from there, things steadily progressed for me. I have got some brilliant opportunities through it, and have met some brilliant like minded people because of it.

Twitter has resulted in not only the growth of my blog, but also me as a person. The support on Twitter is incredibly strong and really shows that kindness is still in this world. When I was having treatment back in June '13 for an overactive thyroid I couldn't be with my little girl or anyone else for three weeks, as I was quarantined. But Twitter, and more specifically the friends I have made through it, kept me company for all that time and really picked me up and kept my spirits high.

Recently I've been to a number of meet ups, where I finally got to put faces and voices to the names I communicate with quite regularly but may live on the other side of the country. Contrary to that, I now have a regular contributor to the blog thanks to Twitter, Eileen is someone I consider a friend but we have never met in person but we hope to change that this summer. Twitter can bring people together in the most unlikely of ways and I wish I had embraced it sooner, but it's never too late!

LilliWhiteRose x

Blog: *http://lilliwhiterose.blogspot.ie/*

Twitter: *@Lilliwhiterose*

Facebook: *https://www.Facebook.com/Lilliwhiterose*

#IrishBizParty at work | Calligraphy | Personalised and Unique Gift

by **Jagdeep Sahans**

I am part of an on-line business community called *#IrishBizParty* founded by *Samantha Kelly* who I'd met through Twitter just over two years ago. You might remember her from *Dragon's Den*. She is quite the genius when it comes to using Twitter has a marketing tool. Sam runs the hashtag IrishBizParty on Twitter on Wednesday evenings 9pm to 11pm.

I was away from social media networking for a good few months and decided it was time to dip my toes back into social media networking via the *#IrishBizParty* only to discover it had grown a lot!!! Outstanding work Sam! I thought to myself. It was fast and furious, I was finding it hard to keep up with the *#IrishBizParty* stream when I got a lovely tweet from Helena Tubridy of *Fertility Expert* saying that she had sent me a query! For me, receiving a calligraphy enquiry is an example of the *#IrishBizParty* at work!

Helena was looking for a unique and special gift for a friend of her's who had just been installed as a Canon and using Calligraphy to produce this gift was the perfect answer for her.

This is what Helena says about working with me:

"I had concerns about working with you remotely but this was overcome with the "work in progress" photo's which was lovely.

Your meticulous attention to the artwork embellishing the letters is wonderful, a masterpiece of precision and design. The address label was an added, generous bonus and is a work of art in itself which wowed the receiver. The piece was well-presented and delivered swiftly, with attention to safety and tracking. You were clear on pricing and timing. I would be delighted to recommend you to produce a lovely unique gift with marvellous detailing."

Wedding Favours

by <u>Jagdeep Sahans</u>

Armelle & I met through Twitter via the *#SMEcommunity* Armelle runs a *French Bakery* in Kilcullen and she has supplied Macaron's (which are mighty tasty) for all our off-line gatherings. It was at one of these off-line gathering's that this story starts.

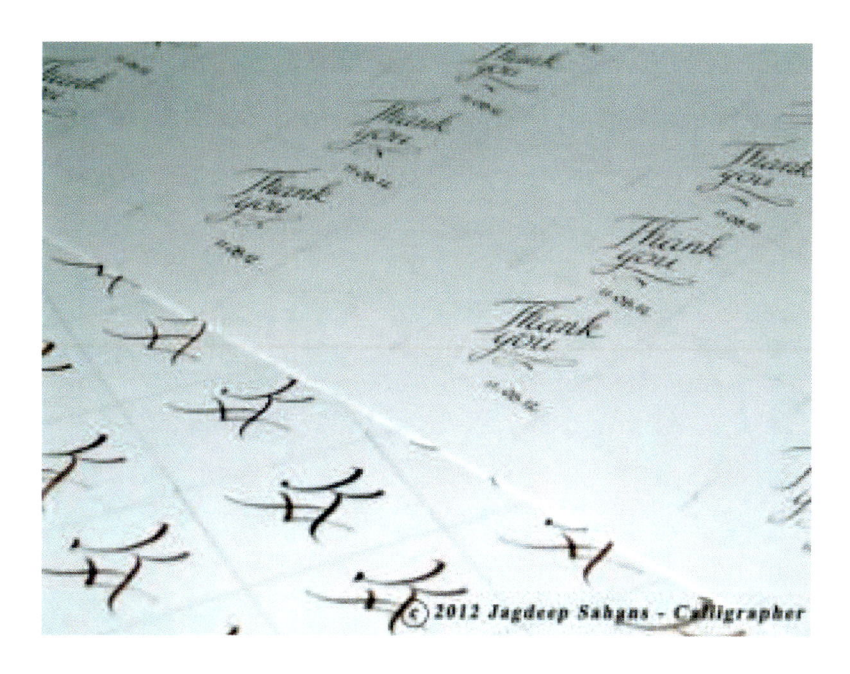

We were at the screening of *@funkygoddessirl* making her pitch to the Irish *Dragon's* when *@armelleskitchen* and *@kennyrorie* mentioned that they'd like to use my Calligraphy as part of their wedding day. (What a lovely compliment I thought & let it be at that. Expecting no more.) But a few weeks or maybe even a couple of months later *@armelleskitchen* tweets that she really did want to use my Calligraphy. I said well in that case lets get creative… we started throwing a few ideas around. The norm's were covered Kenny's sister was making hand-made invitations and the place cards were being supplied by the venue. Short of writing their vows or a table plan or service booklet I was running out of ideas. Then with one of those light-bulb moments Armelle came up with the idea of a Thank you type label that could be used with *@PurityBelle*'s Hand-poured scented candle. What a simple and unique way of using Calligraphy & a collaboration – lovely!

Armelle was going to bake lots of *Macaron*'s for *The Eiffel Tower* and the flavours – I think they were Pistachio, Strawberry & Vanilla which were delicious and translated to pink, green & cream. Our colour scheme sorted. So working with

Armelle & Kenny we came up with a simple flourished monogram for the front & inside "Thank you" with the date of the wedding threaded with raffia & tied to Cliona's candles.

And here is the end result. *Purity Belle's* beautiful hand-poured scented candles with a Hand-made hand-written "Thank you" card.
Photo taken by *David McAuley Photographer*

Have you ever wondered what the blinkers you are going to do next in life?

by Paul Dunphy
https://Twitter.com/pauldunphy

I have.

One minute I was going flat out 24/7 at a full-time media and communications job, the next I was on the psychiatrist's couch - well, not quite the psychiatrist's couch (though I wouldn't mind jumping on the psychiatrist's couch if the right man came along!) - trying to figure out where my work/life balance had gone wrong.

Something had to give - **ME**. I needed a change - and a challenge. Plus, I was the size of a whale from being deskbound for 14 years. (Well, maybe a large dolphin rather than a whale. Actually, let's go for a 'baby whale'!)

So, once I got a new exercise routine in place (now I'm not the size of any form of whale, I'm a sleek panther in fact!) I dipped my toe in the water, in a manner of speaking. I tried out a few different things such as writing - my first short story will be published soon! - going on radio to review films - yes on the Tom Dunne Show, with Marian Keyes - and chocolate tasting for Cadbury Ireland. (True fact!)

However, something else was always calling me ... and that was Twitter!

Up to that point in my life, I had always used Twitter for work, but now I had time to use it for fun, and so I did.

And, boy, what fun was had and continues to be had! I've had tweets from Jackie Collins, Kevin Bacon, Stephen Fry, and twice from THE Cher, to name but a few! Given that I'm prone to boldness and whimsy, Twitter was made for me. One day, while having some such fun, I came across the *@tweetinggoddess* and instantly liked Sam due to the smiley account picture *(the pic is important folks!)*. We chatted and soon became pals.

It was soon after that, that I realised that I wanted to combine my fun side and my media skills. I wanted to be truer to myself. That's when I decided to become a 'social media curator'. What the Dickens is a 'social media curator', you might be wondering! Well, a social media curator is someone who takes care of people's Twitter and Facebook when they don't have time to do so themselves or don't have the necessary know-how.

So with encouragement from Sam and the *#irishbizparty* network, I set myself up with a web page *www.pauldunphyesquire.com* and launched my social media curating career. It's been 'all go' since! I run the *@irishbizparty* and *@britishbizparty* Twitter accounts. I recently 'live' tweeted at the first hugely successful *#irishbizparty* conference and I am just about to take on a new 'client'.

I took the gamble and so far it has paid off. I couldn't have done it without the help, support and sassiness from Sam. She truly is a goddess!

Now I must get back to Twitter. I need to reply to Lionel Richie (Hello is it me you're looking for?!)....

The dark side of Twitter

I would be lying if I didn't let you all know that there is a dark side to Twitter. Because everything happens so fast and people are quick to jump on the bandwagon this can work both ways. There is a dark side and there are horrible, toxic people out there (just like in real life)

On the internet, a *troll* is a person who sows discord on the Internet by starting arguments or upsetting people, by posting messages in an online community (such as a forum, or blog) with the deliberate intent of provoking readers into an emotional response or of otherwise disrupting normal on-topic discussion. (source: *Wikipedia definition*)

I have many experiences of this. They didn't really start until I had reached over 5,000 followers. And it was when I was starting to do well. They have said things which initially upset me and it actually made me lose sleep too. I couldn't understand why these 'people' were being so cruel. But with Trolls there is no logic and they have no values or reasons for doing these things. So there is no intelligent way of engaging with them.

My job and why I do it has been slagged off. (Not linking my name directly of course) I have been called a con artist (as I charge people to run their Twitter accounts – which lots of agencies do) I was just an easy target as I was one woman on my own. Even the *#Irishbizparty* hashtag has been slagged off and not by just anyone, by people who are actually well known with lots of followers! (Mind you, the actual hashtag wasn't tagged in the tweet of course)

I say, if you haven't got something nice to say, don't say anything at all.

My advice is BLOCK and IGNORE. You can also report abuse to Twitter – Go to your settings and click on 'help' there are lots of sections there such as 'Policies and Violations' where you can report users for abuse or impersonations etc..

Some of you might remember the *#SlaneGirl* hashtag which was trending in Ireland. Well I saw the hashtag trending, so clicked but once I realized what was going on I decided I wouldn't click on the 'photos' just as my way of doing the honourable thing. If I clicked on the photo I felt I would be guilty of abusing this lady's dignity. But then I realized, the fact that I clicked on the hashtag does that make me guilty as everyone else? I was so nosey I had to see what it was all about. Makes you think eh?

Basically I think what happened (not sure cos I didn't continue to read or click on the photos) was there was a girl apparently giving oral sex to a man or men at a recent concert and photos were taken that were shared all over the internet. Now don't get me wrong, I am not a prude or innocent in any way I can assure you, but I noticed that the main hashtag that was trending was *#SlaneGirl...* so what happened to the man/men who also took part in the act?

I even feel that writing about this is perhaps giving it attention that makes me guilty of 'getting involved in some way' but I just wanted to point out that although Twitter is wonderful in so many ways, there is a dark side. There are horrible people out there who really don't think before they tweet. They knock people and slag people off without thinking about the person on the receiving end of their words.

Having been targeted by Trolls myself and even bullied in school I know what it feels like. And although this young lady did what she did and was unfortunate that her photo was taken, can you imagine the shame she might be feeling now? We all make mistakes, I challenge anyone to truthfully tell me that they have never ever had a regret in their life that made them feel ashamed or embarrassed. This girl was just unlucky in that she lives in an era that everything is photographed & shared so quickly. In my day, we didn't even have mobiles!

I for one didn't click on the photo as it really is none of my business and I hope she wasn't hurting too much over it. This is the side of Twitter that can suck you in and it is easy to get involved in slagging matches. I have to say I am guilty of it myself in the past. Just wanted to say:

Think before you Tweet!